GIFT

To:
_____

From:
_____

Date:
_____

Occasion:
_____

GIVE ME Beauty

21 Days of Beauty for Ashes:
A Study of Scriptural Truths for Breakthrough

CYNTHIA F. ALBERT

Scriptures are taken from *The Holy Bible,* King James Version
Scriptures marked NLT are taken from *The Holy Bible*, New Living Translation, copyright © 1996, 2004, 2015 by Tyndale House Foundation. Used by permission of Tyndale House Publishers Inc., Carol Stream, Illinois 60188. All rights reserved.

Print ISBN: 978-0-9997844-1-9

Editing by William and Mary Barker and Pastor Marie Wade
Cover design by Lisa Hainline
Interior design by Steve Plummer / spbookdesign.com
Published by Cynthia Forrest Albert

TABLE of CONTENTS

Introduction
How to use this Bible Study

*B*ELOVED, THIS BOOK is designed to challenge you or a small group to 21 days of daily morning devotions for 21 minutes. The Scriptures selected will promote a positive mindset towards the thoughts you have about yourself, others, your healing, and the life-giving, transforming power of God's Word. Your dedication to 21 days of morning devotion, prayer and fasting will allow time for self-exploration, positive affirmations, Bible reading, and suggested prayer; all placed together to build and strengthen your faith.

The healing you are looking for within yourself, others, and those that you are led to intercede for will come by faith— *Nothing will be impossible for you during these 21 days.* (Refer to Matthew 17:14-21.)

There are some things that God must deliver us from that have been with us since childhood. Often our internal battles are won through the power of wisdom, generosity, spiritual truth, forgiveness, realism, expressing gratitude, striving for healthy relationships, developing pleasant surroundings: work, home, church, etc., and helping others. *Then some emotional issues will only come out through the Power of Fasting and Praying,* according to Mark 9:29.

Let us begin this informative and blessed journey of ours in the Book of Daniel, starting at Chapter 10. We find him praying over Jerusalem for three weeks, 21 days of eating only fruits, nuts and grains. His diet during this time frame was considered plain: no meat, no seasoning, nor strong drink. As you continue to read the chapter, in verses 12 through 14, it is explained when Daniel decided to humble himself and pray. Then the Lord set out to come to him but was delayed by a demonic force, but Michael the archangel intervened to help. After receiving heavenly aid, Daniel was able to understand the vision that had to do with future events. You may have been seeking your emotional healing or something else's for a while, but now you have decided you need heavenly aid for the answer. The understanding or revelation you have been waiting for will come when you begin to fast and pray.

If you decide to fast during your time of study and are under the care of a physician it is strongly recommended to clear the practice with your medical practitioner.

Ask, and it shall be given, seek, and you shall find, knock and the door shall be opened. (Please review Matthew 7:7-8 and Luke 11:9.) The door to your healing, transformation, and deliverance is just a prayer away. You are challenged during this time to go BOLDLY before the throne and with grace ask your Heavenly Father for the healing you need. Ask Him to permeate your personality, to deliver you from your fears, uproot your pride, tear down negative thoughts, remove your worries and uplift your spirit. The following steps will assist you or a small group.

Are You Ready?

STEP 1 - Set aside 21 minutes every morning for 21 days where you can pray. In 21 days or 3 weeks, you will have found a new prayer habit while also refining your character. During this time the Holy Spirit may lead you to fast for 21, 7, or 3 days.

Step 2 - Pray with confidence, study the Word, meditate on the Scriptures, seek forgiveness, and talk to the Holy Spirit. Be determined to engage at new levels despite your emotional state.

Step 3 - Don't Give Up! Keep Going! You may be tempted to stop, become distracted, or made to feel hopeless. You must believe this is the season for the change you have been seeking. Don't give into the lies or negative self-talk that is racing through your mind. *According to 2 Corinthians 10:3-5, we use God's mighty weapons, not worldly weapons, to knock down the strongholds of human reasoning and to destroy false arguments.* We destroy every proud obstacle that keeps people from knowing God and entering a more intimate relationship with Him. We capture our rebellious thoughts and teach them to obey Christ, God's Word.

Step 4 - Tell others about the 21-day challenge. Ask others to join you in prayer and fasting to support you. Encourage family members and friends to take this challenge with you.

Step 5 - Find an accountability partner. An accountability partner is recommended if you choose to do the problem as an independent study. Your partner must be someone to follow up with you to ensure you are on target to complete this survey of scriptures in 21 days and to pray with you. This relationship should be built upon trust, encouragement, wisdom and sound doctrine. Once you have identified a person, pray before asking them to partner with you during this study time. After you have prayed and feel comfortable, proceed with this committed relationship. However, once the relationship has started and you discover the connection is not adding value to your spiritual journey, it is okay to express your concern politely and continue the study independently. If you elected to be a part of a small group, your facilitator will check on you and be available to pray and answer questions.

The Study Format is Easy!!!

It consists of:

Scripture – Sacred writings of Christianity that focus on God's view of BEAUTY.

Timeless Beauty Tips – BEAUTY tips based on scripture that will never go out of STYLE.

Daily Affirmation – POSITIVE statement that promotes a healthy positive mental status.

Makeover Scriptures – Scriptures that can do a COMPLETE TRANSFORMATION in your life by the power of the Holy Spirit.

Let's Nail It! – a time of SELF-EXPLORATION of the Scriptures you are encouraged to meditate on for that day.

Polished Prayer – Prayers that are written to refine you into the BEAUTIFUL WOMAN God has purposed you to be.

Declaration – A daily statement or proclamation.

At the end of each week, the reader is encouraged to

Powder Up,
Brush on more, and
Add a little more Color! –

meaning meditate more on God's Word according to:

Psalm 1:1-3 *Oh, the joys of those who do not follow the advice of the wicked, or stand around with sinners, or join in with mockers. But they delight in the law of the Lord, meditating on it day and night. They are like trees planted along the riverbank, bearing fruit each season. Their leaves never wither, and they prosper in all they do.* (NLT)

Psalm 19:14 *Let the words of my mouth and the meditation of my heart be acceptable in your sight, O LORD, my rock and my Redeemer.* (NLT)

Psalm 104:34 *Let my meditation be pleasing to Him; As for me, I shall be glad in the LORD. My meditation of him shall be sweet: I will be glad in the LORD.* (NLT)

Philippians 4:8 *Finally, brethren, whatever is true, whatever is honorable, whatever is right, whatever is pure, whatever is lovely, whatever is of good repute, if there is any excellence and if anything worthy of praise, dwell on these things.* (NLT)

SEEK THE LORD EARLY

Week One

O God, thou art my God; *early will I seek* thee: my soul thirsteth for thee, my flesh longeth for thee in a dry and thirsty land, where no water is...

PSALM 63:1 KJV

Day 1

To appoint unto them that mourn in Zion, to give unto
them beauty for ashes, the oil of joy for mourning,
the garment of praise for the spirit of heaviness;
that they might be called trees of righteousness, the
planting of the Lord, that he might be glorified.

ISAIAH 61:3

What is left after a dead body has been cremated? Ashes: a gray to black powdery residue. Some would say dust. Who do you know personally that takes an interest in a dead body, let alone someone's cremated ashes? God does. He can take the residue of our dead past and offenses that leave us grieving, oppressed and joyless, then restore us completely. You see, God's ways are different from our human methods. He takes us through the fiery furnace of life's trials and tribulations to burn us into ashes and miraculously change us into something ***beautiful***—a display of His splendor!

Makeover Scriptures: Isaiah 61, Psalm 4:1, Psalm 18:6, Psalm 27:14, Psalm 34:14, Psalm 107:41-43; Psalm 113:7

Timeless Beauty Tip #1:
You are CROWNED with BEAUTY!

✳ ✳ ✳

Today, allow God to cremate you so He can turn you into the BEAUTIFUL WOMAN He purposed you to be!

✳ ✳ ✳

Let's Naut!

1. According to today's Scripture, what does God want to do for you?

_____

_____

_____

_____

2. In exchange for grief, mourning, and heaviness, what does He want to give you?

_____

_____

_____

_____

3. How are we like trees? Do you know other Scriptures that use trees as a metaphor?

4. Read 2 Corinthians 10:3-6. What negative emotions, habits or thoughts are you willing to burn away over the next 21 days?

Polished Prayer:

Lord, you promised in your Word to change our lives right-side-up for you to be glorified and for us to be planted in righteousness. We embrace the transformation and the pain that comes with not remaining the same. He lifts us out of afflictions and shuts the mouth or our enemies; therefore, we can rejoice! Holy Spirit, move us from a dolorous state of sinking in misery or grief.

* * *

**Today, I command
depression, oppression,
sadness, disappointment, and
discouragement to GO because
I am DROP DEAD GORGEOUS!**

* * *

Day 2

Do ye look on things after the outward appear-
ance? If any man trust to himself that he is
Christ's, let him of himself think this again, that,
as he is Christ's, even so are we Christ's.

2 CORINTHIANS 10:7

ob approached Mary at church and stated, "You decided not to pick up items for the toy drive with everyone. Oh, you did not want to lift any heavy items?" Mary smiled and politely shared that she decided to stay at the church to provide phone coverage while the other ministry team picked up the toys. Early that same day Mary had encountered Sandy's negative undertones. When she stated, "Oh, Mary won't participate in that group event," the other party in the conversation asked, "How do you know that?" We cannot control adverse, unexpected, casual conversations, but only our position in Christ will help us handle how we deal with each situation.

Makeover Scriptures: Philippians 2:5-11; 2 Corinthians 10:1-8

Timeless Beauty Tip #2:
Your MIND belongs to Christ!

❀ ❀ ❀

Father God, renew our minds and adjust how we think about ourselves and others.

❀ ❀ ❀

Let's Nail IT!

1. According to this passage of Scripture, others have been in a situation of negativity, even considered in a negative light, by others in the church. How was Paul being viewed by other believers?

2. At this moment, how are you allowing others to define who you are with their words? If you are, what can you do to renew your mind?

3. Are you allowing your negative emotional state to define who you are? If so, describe how.

4. The point Paul was trying to get across to the believers is that it didn't matter what they thought about him as a Christian, we all belong to Christ, even those who you assume are Christians may be acting out of godly character. He was encouraging the believers to capture their toxic, harmful, stinking thinking and walk in the power and authority God has given us! How did Paul respond to his letter to the Corinthians?

Polished Prayer:

Lord, forgive us for forming negative thoughts about our brothers and sisters in Christ Jesus. The difference needed is our new perspective of life in YOU. Lord, align our thoughts, words and body language with your will for our lives through Christ Jesus. Help us to avoid being opinionated, and making subtle innuendos about others. Holy Spirit, transition us from operating out of our flesh to warring in the spiritual battle for our minds.

✽ ✽ ✽

Strongholds in my mind, will, and emotions are being smashed, broken, and destroyed in Jesus's Name.

✽ ✽ ✽

Day 3

For ye were sometimes darkness, but now are ye
light in the Lord: walk as children of light.

EPHESIANS 5:8

God's light is glowing inside of us; therefore, no situation, person, physical condition, thought, or emotion shall force us off course. God is leading us; therefore, we do not have to be distracted by the evil around us. Our light should shine brightly, eliminating every dark, dreary, low hanging cloud hovering over us because the SON never stops shining.

Makeover Scriptures: Ephesians 5:1-14; Romans 8:35-39; Acts 3:19; 2 Corinthians 5:17; Psalm 103:12; Mark 11:25

Timeless Beauty Tip #3:
You are SHINING!

❋   ❋   ❋

Today, no matter what is going on, I am determined to get BRIGHTER!

❋   ❋   ❋

Let's Nail IT!

1. In order to walk as children of light, list the things we should not be a part of after reading Ephesians 5:1-4:

_____

_____

_____

_____

_____

_____

2. What should we do to expose the deeds of darkness?

_____

_____

_____

_____

_____

3. What does Ephesians 5:14 mean to you?

Polished Prayer:

Lord, we thank you for being our light and our salvation. Your light transfigures our being by penetrating the hardness of our hearts, exposing the sin in our lives, and cutting through the lies the enemy has erected over the years. Prepare us physically, mentally, and spiritually to walk as children of light as you surround us with songs of deliverance. Holy Spirit, shine the right radiance we need to succeed from the INSIDE OUT!

✳ ✳ ✳

**Striving to let MY Life Shine,
I rebuke the works of evil
that may be hidden in and all
around me!!!**

✳ ✳ ✳

Day 4

But let it be the hidden man of the heart, in that which is not corruptible, even the ornament of a meek and quiet spirit, which is in the sight of God of great price.

For after this manner in the old time the holy women also, who trusted in God, adorned themselves, being in subjection unto their own husbands.

1 PETER 3:4-5

Do you have school pictures and memories from when you were a little girl? Photos that show your hair neatly decorated with ribbons and bows? Sometimes the style was to your liking and at other times, not. The Word of God challenges us to practice adorning our inner man with God's Word since our outer beauty is fleeting. Ultimately, God is pleased with a mild temperament, so, purpose in your heart to be a God Pleaser.

Makeover Scriptures: Philippians 4:6-7; Ephesians 4:1-3; Matthew 6:14-15

Timeless Beauty Tip #4:
You are GENTLE, QUIET, and SUBMITTED!

❋ ❋ ❋

Today, adorn yourself with calmness, forgiveness, and long-suffering in order to have healthy relationships with others.

❋ ❋ ❋

Let's Nail IT!

1. Currently, how do you adorn yourself to prepare to face the various roles in your life?

_____

_____

_____

_____

2. Assess how you accept the authority of your husband based on this Scripture. If you are not married, evaluate how you respond to authority figures. Do you automatically react out of your emotions, or do you feel comfortable around those in authority over you? Is it out of fear or another negative emotional stance?

_____

_____

_____

3. How do you know if your style of communication is received by other? Especially when you are engaged in conversation with those who have an authoritative role in your life. Is what you are doing effective and, if not, what can you do differently? For example, do you roll your eyes or shrug your shoulder to express doubt or indifference?

4. Are you a "God Pleaser" or a "Man Pleaser"?

Polished Prayer:

Lord, thank you for giving us a living Helper, the Holy Spirit. As we adorn ourselves with God's Word, Holy Spirit, strengthen us to walk in the imperishable beauty of a gentle disposition because this is precious in our Father's sight. Let us not be anxious, unforgiving, or impatient as we do good in our relationships with others. At this moment, we decide fear and intimidation will not overpower our decision-making process by repeatedly ruminating about what others might say or do.

* * *

I take *Bold* precious steps towards success from the inside out in every relationship I encounter.

* * *

Day 5

They looked unto him, and were lightened:
and their faces were not ashamed.

PSALM 34:5

So much happened in Teresa's life, it all seemed like one big tear. In one year, she faced the shame of foreclosure, her husband left for a younger woman, a son experimented with drugs, and friends betrayed her. In the midst of it all, she also had to look for a place to live while holding it together day after day while being bullied on the job! You may be in a similar dilemma like Teresa's, or worse, yet hang in there and look to HIM! When distracted by life circumstances, shame and other negative emotions tend to be magnified. Trouble will arise in our lives. Nevertheless, God has promised His presence, comfort, joy, and peace if we continue to seek HIM and be willing to experience HIS glory, He will uphold us.

Makeover Scriptures: Psalm 25, Psalm 37, Ephesians 5:27

Timeless Beauty Tip #5:

You are RADIANT!

❊ ❊ ❊

Today, direct your thoughts towards God's Word and do not allow shame to win!

❊ ❊ ❊

Let's Nail IT!

1. What event(s) in your life have caused you to experience the negative emotion of shame?

_____

_____

_____

_____

_____

2. How have you responded to this negative emotion?

_____

_____

_____

_____

_____

3. According to today's study, what has God promised you?

4. How can you practice being radiant today, according to Ephesians 5:27?

Polished Prayer:

Lord, I thank you for being with us in the midst of our troubles as we paddle through the waves of life. Allow us to rise and shine in every situation we must face. We stand on the promise that you will put our enemies to shame. You will vindicate us. As we center our attention on Jesus, pride and self-centeredness will not win. Holy Spirit, remove shyness, lying, and a victim mentality. Let us not hold any grudges and help us break other bad habits that block our real personality.

Lord, you are everything; therefore, strengthen us to walk in boldness, courage, and victory!!!!

* * *

I RADIATE elegance in all life circumstances!

* * *

Day 6

So shall the king greatly desire thy beauty: for
he is thy Lord; and worship thou him.

PSALM 45:11

Are your thoughts tainted by all the scars of abuse, misuse of your body, abortion, unforgiveness, drugs, rejection, and hurt and pain stuffed deep inside? Your partner, spouse, or significant other like your external being. Unfortunately, your internal trash keeps oozing out and emitting an offensive odor. You think your problems are unique to this relationship. Then you slowly begin to realize you are having problems with ALL relationships.

Makeover Scriptures: Romans 12:1; Psalm 8:1; Psalm 100:4; John 4:21-24; James 4:8

Timeless Beauty Tip #6:
You are WORSHIP!

❋ ❋ ❋

Today, I present my body as a living sacrifice holy and acceptable unto you which is MY REASONABLE SERVICE.

❋ ❋ ❋

Let's Nail IT!

1. List the ways you currently worship God:

2. What are you doing that is hindering your ability to worship God?

3. List the ways you revere and honor others (husband, supervisors, and friends):

4. What is hindering you from revering and honoring others?

5. What are some additional things you can do to worship/ honor God and show respect to others?

6. Meditate on your favorite Scriptures pertaining to worship and honoring God. What is speaking to your heart about to them?

Polished Prayer:

Instruct us as we choose to shine from the inside out and to always worship and honor you. Reveal negative attitudes we have towards others and life circumstances that we cannot control. We need a refreshing, a fresh outpouring of your Spirit. Teach us to *Let go and Live*!!! Guide us as we venture into new ways of reverencing YOU and showing respect to ourselves and others. Forgive us for choosing the posture of striving to be equal to you, to be heard, and to boast our opinions.

* * *

The change I desperately want to see starts on a Bended Knee!

* * *

Day 7

*I will praise thee; for I am fearfully and won-
derfully made; marvellous are thy works;
and that my soul knoweth right well.*

PSALM 139:14

Recently, my friends and I went to an outdoor farmers market. There were vendors selling fresh fruit and veg-etables, honey, kettle popcorn, handmade jewelry, etc. One of the many tables grabbed our attention. It displayed hand knitted wrist warmers, fingerless gloves, softly knit cowls and cozy, colored scarfs and beanies. Just like the knit-ter's luxuriously cozy colored items, God created the inner-most part of us. Therefore, we can take the dilemma of our internal mess we find ourselves entangled in and bring it to Him. Yes, HE knows we are fragile, yet He made us delicate, but elegant.

Makeover Scriptures: Psalm 139

Timeless Beauty Tip #7:
You are KNITTED TOGETHER!

❊ ❊ ❊

**Today, despite all the triggers that
may be alarming on the inside, I am
FEARFULLY AND WONDERFULLY made
and marvelous are your works!**

❊ ❊ ❊

Let's Nail IT!

1. What are your triggers and negative responses to external events that cause you to respond based on past traumatic events?

_____

_____

_____

_____

_____

2. What negative responses have you observed in someone else? How will you respond differently after meditating upon this Scripture?

_____

_____

_____

_____

3. Look at Psalm 139:16. What does it mean to you?

Polished Prayer:

Lord, forgive us for trying to put your creation back together again without the Creator. Forgive us for our old emotional responses when faced with certain tones, facial expressions, and body languages. No longer will we respond out of our traumatic past with hurt, pain, and embarrassment. We believe you can knit the torn delicate pieces of our being back together again. We are running this race with confidence that He who hath begun a good work and will complete it!!!

* * *

I decree and declare I am FIT
and FLARING!!!

* * *

Powder UP!

And be not conformed to this world; but be ye transformed by the renewing of your mind, that ye may prove what is that good, and acceptable, a perfect will of God. Romans 12:2

Finally, brethren, whatsoever things are true, whatsoever things are honest, whatsoever things are just, whatsoever things are pure, whatsoever things are lovely, whatsoever things are of good report; if there be any virtue, and if there be any praise , think on these things. Philippians 4:8

For which cause we faint not; but though our outward man perish, yet the inward man is renewed day by day. 2 Corinthians 4:16

Thy word have I hid in mine heart, that I might not sin against thee. Psalms 119:11

Let the word of Christ dwell in you richly in all wisdom; teaching and admonishing one another in psalms and hymns and spiritual songs, singing with grace in your hearts to the Lord. Colossians 3:16

PRAY WITH CONFIDENCE

Week Two

Let us therefore come boldly unto the throne of grace that we may obtain mercy, and find grace to help in time of need.

HEBREWS 4:16

Day 8

He hath made everything beautiful in his time: also he hath set the world in their heart, so that no man can find out the work that God maketh from the beginning to the end.

ECCLESIASTES 3:11

As we age, we may feel behind the curveball especially if significant events did not happen in our twenties, thirties, or forties, etc.; for example, if we did not complete high school or college because we got pregnant. Everything has a time to be beautiful. This includes the situations that occur in our lives. We must realize beauty is always there, but the possessor and the beholder must discover it. The beauty of an education and a prosperous career was always there, but due to dropping out of high school, we may not see it until we mature later on in life.

Makeover Scriptures: Ecclesiastes 3:1-11; Romans 8:28

Timeless Beauty Tip #8:
You are ON TIME!

❋ ❋ ❋

There are no missed opportunities in our lives, only NEW BEGINNINGS!

❋ ❋ ❋

Let's Nail IT!

1. In what ways do you feel life has passed you by?

2. What can you say about the events you have been expecting to happen, but have not?

3. Write a testimony of how all things are working together for the good, according to Romans 8:28.

Polished Prayer:

Lord, I thank you that we have a season coming and we will be on time! Lord, search out the gifts and talents hidden inside of us so that we can discover our divine potential. We are treasures hidden in earthen vessels. Lord, reveal to us who you created us to be and what you have designed for us to accomplish on this earth. Forgive us for being resistant to change by being gripped by our past, being afraid, procrastinating and dreaming, and not moving by faith.

✿ ✿ ✿

Today, I decree and declare life happens and I have a FRESH START!

✿ ✿ ✿

Day 9

But if we walk in the light, as he is in the light, we have fellowship one with another, and the blood of Jesus Christ his Son cleanseth us from all sin.

1 JOHN 1:7

Conflict occurs when one or both parties are not walking in the light, but we must remember that we are all under HIS grace and mercy. The blood of Jesus cleanses us from all sin. Discord is an opportunity to respond in love, forgiveness, or repentance for our inexperienced or immature responses. Conflict is a time to admit being out of fellowship with Christ which causes disunity among others.

Makeover Scripture: Matthew 23, Psalm 51, Proverbs 4:23; Psalm 138:23

Timeless Beauty Tip #9:

You are CLEAN!

❋ ❋ ❋

Today, I admit it is time to do some spring cleaning from this internal mess I am experiencing in my life!

❋ ❋ ❋

Let's Nail IT!

1. Think of a time in the past or perhaps recently that you experienced conflict. How did you behave in the situation?

2. How did you exhibit God's grace and mercy?

3. What could you have done differently?

Polished Prayer:

Lord, thank you that we are cleansed from all our sins, and we are in fellowship with you. We each admit being a BEAUTIFUL MESS. Externally, we are on point, but internally we feel like we are bouncing all over the place. Forgive us for our immature emotional responses to discord, incompatibility, and disagreement. Turn our eyes inward as we take our errors and shortcomings quietly to YOU in prayer. Holy Spirit, guide and comfort us as we attempt to understand one another and move forward from offense.

*** *** ***

I AM COVERED by the blood of Jesus and walking in fellowship with HIM and others!

*** *** ***

Day 10

For ye are all the children of God by faith in Christ Jesus.
GALATIANS 3:26

To what have you given your all? There are several things that we can submerge ourselves into: securing a job, pursuing an education, watching sports, reading, watching movies, making money, spending time with family, dating, hanging out with friends, playing video games, listening to music, surfing the internet or engulfing ourselves into the latest app. All of these activities can provide temporary satisfaction, but when you extend your faith to believe that you can be eternally satisfied forever with Jesus, the other things become superficial.

Makeover Scripture: Ephesians 3:16-17; 1 Peter 4:8; Proverbs 3:3-4; Proverbs 31:25; Colossians 3:12; Psalm 143:8; 1 John 4:18

Timeless Beauty Tip #10:

You are CLOTHED IN LOVE!

✿ ✿ ✿

Beloved, allow God to veil you with His Love!

✿ ✿ ✿

Let's Nail IT!

1. According to Scripture, a Christian's attire should represent Jesus Christ. List some of those Christ-like attributes:

_____

_____

_____

_____

_____

2. Write a brief testimony of what God's eternal Love and Protection means to you:

_____

_____

_____

_____

_____

Polished Prayer:

Lord, we aim to let receive your love and faithfulness lead us in everything we do. Desiring to be a living epistle, let grace, love, and charity abide in our hearts. As we trust you, allow your Word to come to us throughout the day to show us the way. Walking by faith, strengthen us to care for others deeply because love covers a multitude of sins. Lord, we submerge ourselves in your love because YOU are love; therefore, we are in love.

✼ ✼ ✼

**Today, I decree and declare
my Wardrobe is Love and I am
DECKED OUT!!**

✼ ✼ ✼

Day 11

Thine heart was lifted up because of thy beauty, thou hast corrupted thy wisdom by reason of thy brightness: I will cast thee to the ground, I will lay thee before kings, that they may behold thee.

Thou hast defiled thy sanctuaries by the multitude of thine iniquities, by the iniquity of thy traffick; therefore will I bring forth a fire from the midst of thee, it shall devour thee, and I will bring thee to ashes upon the earth in the sight of all them that behold thee.

EZEKIEL 28:17-18

The condition of our hearts is what God is concerned about. Things happen to us and for us based on the state of our hearts. Bottom line—sin has consequences. Here are some thoughts to ponder: Have you allowed your beauty to become your downfall? Have you used your beauty to be promiscuous, to be adulterous, to manipulate, to intimidate and negatively influence others? Do you flirt to get or have your way? Do you persuade others with your beauty to be on your side, buy your product, bless you with money, or join your agenda/ministry?

Makeover Scripture: 1 Timothy 3:11; Ephesians 1:18-23; 2 Timothy 3:16

Timeless Beauty Tip #11:
You are WISE!

❊ ❊ ❊

I must take ownership of guarding my Heart!

❊ ❊ ❊

Let's Nail IT!

1. In your own words, what do these Scriptures mean to you?

_____

_____

_____

_____

2. What are the consequences of pride (sin), according to 1 Timothy 3:11?

_____

_____

_____

_____

3. A divided heart is just like sensitive skin. There is a solution. Matt 22:37 challenges us to love the Lord our God with all our hearts, and with all our souls, and with all our minds. Are you separating yourself from God's love? If so, in what way?

Polished Prayer:

Lord, continue to show us the condition of our hearts. Remove the following intruders: pride, offense, manipulation, and gossip. Reveal other sins like greed, envy, and jealousy that slip in without our knowledge, and are bottled up, concealed and wrapped tightly within. You are the only one who tries the heart and searches it out. The condition of our hearts impacts our ability to receive all that you have for us. Holy Spirit, lead us down the path of a life of happiness and integrity. We avail to be serious, wise, and faithful in all things. Forgive us for allowing our thoughts, selfishness, and stunning features to guide us away from your presence.

* * *

Today, I decree and declare I am ENLIGHTENED!

* * *

Day 12

As a jewel of gold in a swine's snout, so is a fair woman which is without discretion.

PROVERBS 11:22

1. Define the following words:

A. Discreet

B. Deceit

C. Hypocrite

D. Jealousy

Makeover Scriptures: 1 Peter 2:1; Proverbs 19:13; Proverbs 21:9; Proverbs 21:19; 2 Corinthians 5:17

Timeless Beauty Tip #12:
You are DISCREET!

❋ ❋ ❋

Today, I work on being agreeable enjoyable, pleasant, nice, charming, delightful, friendly, good-natured, sociable and congenial.

❋ ❋ ❋

Let's Nail IT!

1. The following are some questions to ponder. Do you roll your eyes? Do you suck your teeth? Do you pout? Does your tone offend others? Are you easily offended? Do you point your finger? Do you stomp your feet and storm off? Do you curse? Are you two-faced? Do your beliefs and behavior agree? Do you resent others success? Do you gossip?

2. What bad habit(s) do you need help getting rid of?

Polished Prayer:

There are behaviors we need to discard by confessing they have contaminated our relationship with YOU for a long time. We have hurt and the pain has been excruciating. We come across as annoying or a nuisance. Holy Spirit, heal our wounded souls as we pursue living agreeably. These dark shadows have crept into our lives. Willingly we have allowed them to take residence; however, they have been served a 21-day eviction notice.

❋ ❋ ❋

**I decree and declare I am a
New Creature!**

❋ ❋ ❋

Day 13

And God is able to make all grace abound toward you; that ye, always having all sufficiency in all things, may abound to every good work.

2 CORINTHIANS 9:8

Seeking God for everything can seem insurmountable if it is not a task we are accustomed to doing all the time. We can also ask HIM to empower us to live a life of abundance. HE has the protection, love, finances, relationships, and career we need. Our purpose is in HIS hands. Allow HIM to guide you with HIS eye. Release the wheel and allow the Lord to steer you in HIS direction. Stop leaning, depending on yourself and others. Seek HIM for your physical, emotional, relationship, and financial needs.

Makeover Scriptures: Psalm 103; Genesis 39:4, 21

Timeless Beauty Tip #13:
You are SUFFICIENT!

❊ ❊ ❊

Today, I sit quietly and wait for God to provide.

❊ ❊ ❊

Let's Nail IT!

1. What is the Grace of God?

2. What is God's Favor?

3. List ways you seek satisfaction that are not pleasing to God.

4. List things that you are putting before God.

5. Give examples of acts of charity you have expressed recently.

6. What areas of life (Family/Household, Relationships, Career, Education, Finances, Ministry) do you need to trust and believe that God will meet the need?

Polished Prayer:

Lord, we need your grace more than anything right now. We have sought advice and talked about our current problems until we are tired mentally, emotionally, and physically. Lord, we need your strength to be complete, as we exchange our negative stances for the satisfaction we can find in you. Allow your grace to kick in so that we can be sufficient in everything we do.

✳ ✳ ✳

I decree and declare
my SATISFACTION IS
GUARANTEED, an ABUNDANT
LIFE!

✳ ✳ ✳

Day 14

*Rejoice in the Lord, O ye righteous: for
praise is comely for the upright.*

PSALM 33:1

Developing and maintaining a relationship with God may seem odd because He is invisible, but His presence is powerful. The Bible tells us how to enter into His presence in Psalm 100:4: "Enter into his gates with thanksgiving, and into his courts with praise: be thankful unto him, and bless his name." "Sing joyfully unto the Lord" is a bold declaration by making an outward expression of praise to uplift the name of Jesus. The opposite is being bound in our thinking, sitting rigidly in a praise and worship service with arms folded, looking around and being critical of everything that is happening around us. Questioning, does it take all that? Is all that hollering necessary? Is God pleased with this type of behavior? Is this joy genuine? The adjective "comely" is defined by Merriam online dictionary as "pleasing in appearance; pretty or attractive." This expression is usually not a part of our everyday conversations, but this one word describes how God feels about our praise. He is attracted to it. You mean God does not care about our nail, hair, lip or eyeshadow color? No, girlfriend! He is drawn to our praise. God dwells in the midst of our praise. Do you need God to show up in your life? The answer is to praise HIM!

Makeover Scriptures: Psalm 32:11; Psalm 33; Psalm 149:6; 2 Chronicles 20:22

Timeless Beauty Tip #14:
You are ATTRACTIVE!

❉ ❉ ❉

Today, I chose to outwardly express my praise despite how I feel.

❉ ❉ ❉

Let's Nail IT!

1. What does singing joyfully mean to you?

2. Which phrase or word best describes your praise:

    a. Active watcher

    b. Active participant

    c. Radical

3. Define comely:

4. What is hindering your ability to give HIM Radical Praise?

5. What are you willing to do differently to have a more intimate relationship with our heavenly Father?

Polished Prayer:

Religion, ignorance, worldly beliefs, and a critical stance have kept us from giving you the praise that is due to your name. We understand you are attracted to our praise; therefore, forgive us for not giving YOU our best praise. Your Word is full of examples of how people praise you; singing, dancing, clapping, shouting, and lifting up hands. You have promised if we draw nigh unto thee you will draw nigh unto us. Father, I thank you for your promises and stand on them.

* * *

I decree and declare, my
pretty praise is drawing
a powerful God into my
situation.

* * *

Brush on more!

And be renewed in the spirit of your mind.
EPHESIANS 4:23

*Wherefore gird up the loins of your mind, be sober,
and hope to the end for the grace that is to be brought
unto you at the revelation of Jesus Christ.*
1 PETER 1:13

*Be careful for nothing; but in everything by
prayer and supplication with thanksgiving let
your request be made known unto God.*
PHILIPPIANS 4:6-7

*For the weapons of our warfare are not carnal, but mighty
through God to the pulling down of strongholds; Casting
down imaginations, and every high thing that exalteth
itself against the knowledge of God, and bringing into
captivity every thought to the obedience of Christ.*
2 CORINTHIANS 10:4-5

*Set your affection on things above,
not on things on the earth.*
COLOSSIANS 3:2

*And ye shall know the truth, and the
truth shall make you free.*
JOHN 8:32

KEEP ASKING, SEEKING and KNOCKING
Week Three

Ask, and it shall be given to you;
seek, and ye shall find; knock, and
it shall be opened unto you:
8 For every one that asketh receiveth;
and he that seeketh findeth;
and to him that knocketh
it shall be opened.
9 Or what man is there of you, whom if his
son ask bread, will he give him a stone?
10 Or if he ask a fish, will he
give him a serpent?
11 If ye then, being evil, know how to give
good gifts unto your children, how much
more shall your Father which is in heaven
give good things to them that ask him?
12 Therefore all things whatsoever ye would
that men should do to you, do ye even so to
them: for this is the law and the prophets.

MATTHEW 7:7-12

Day 15

Who can find a virtuous woman? for
her price is far above rubies.

PROVERBS 31:10

I am not perfect, I am a wife, I am a mother, I am a grand-mother, I am a homemaker, I am respectful, I am confident, I am secure, I am patient, I am a quiet strength, I am business-minded, I am wise, I am a prayer warrior, I am an investor, I am a writer, I am a mentor, I am a leader, I am victorious, and I am more than a conqueror.

Sorry, you can't see all the beauty in me!!!!!

Makeover Scriptures: Proverbs 31

Timeless Beauty Tip #15:

You are Priceless!

✻ ✻ ✻

Just like strongly colored DIAMONDS I am RARE, but PRICELESS!!!

✻ ✻ ✻

Let's Nail IT!

1. Write out all the qualities within you that make you priceless that you and others may not see.

_____

_____

_____

_____

2. Meditate on Proverbs 31. What verses stand out to you about this Proverbs 31 Woman?

_____

_____

_____

_____

3. Look at Proverbs 31:15. Why was this woman able to accomplish so much? She had help maids and maidens. What three tasks or assignments can you delegate to accomplish your goals?

4. We see this woman's accomplishments and the end results, but what about her process? Butterflies, flowers, and diamonds go through a transformation process. Briefly, share how allowing Jesus into your heart has transformed your life:

Polished Prayer:

We all desire to be that Proverbs 31 Woman, but allow us to see the tasks that are overwhelming us, not in our gift zone and time wasters. Connect us with older and younger women who can come alongside us to assist us in accomplishing our goals. Holy Spirit, guide us as we take an inward look at ourselves, then allow us to see our ravishing, unique qualities that you have exquisitely placed within. Let our light so shine before men, that they may see your good works, and glorify our Father which is in heaven.

* * *

Today, I decree and declare I am OUTSTANDING!!!

* * *

Day 16

For a good tree bringeth not forth corrupt fruit; neither doth a corrupt tree bring forth good fruit.

For every tree is known by his own fruit. For of thorns men do not gather figs, nor of a bramble bush gather the grapes.

A good man out of the good treasure of his heart bringeth forth that which is good; and an evil man out of the evil treasure of his heart bringeth forth that which is evil: for of the abundance of the heart his mouth speaketh.

LUKE 6:43-45

"If you gain weight, I will leave you. All you do is sit in front of that computer eating junk all day. You are worthless. Why don't you do something productive? I told her if she didn't change I was leaving. She knew I would not stay around if she gained weigh I told her that from the beginning."

David blamed everything that was wrong in his relationship with Nancy on Nancy. This is often the case when someone is verbally abusive. They never take responsibility for their actions.

Makeover Scriptures: Psalm 55:21; Psalm 19:4; Proverbs 18:10; Proverbs 29:20; Romans 12:2; Ephesians 4:23; Colossians 3:10

Timeless Beauty Tip #16:
Your FLOW IS FLAWLESS!

✤ ✤ ✤

I purpose my words to be sweet as HONEY!

✤ ✤ ✤

1. Listed below are six toxic ways of communicating. Research and define their meaning:

A. Blaming

B. Name Calling

C. Threats

D. Public Correction and or Teasing

E. Critical Humor

F. Disapproving Attitude (Nonverbal)

2. On a scale of 1 to 10, how would you rate the condition of your heart after meditating on Luke 6:43-45 and looking of the meaning of the words listed above, with1 being Poor and 10 being a Good Heart?

3. What changes can you make to improve your heart rating?

A.

B.

C.

D.

E.

F.

Polished Prayer:

Lord, help us to think before we speak and allow our words to flow flawlessly from our lips to the listener's ears. When we talk, let our words bring wisdom, discernment, and revelation from you. Help our communication style to be free of hate, harshness, offense, slander, and our opinions. Purge our hearts from dead works that are bitter to our souls. Forgive us for exalting our agendas and not exalting your name. Lord, help us to hear what brings understanding, clarity, and knowledge from you.

* * *

**My words are Soothing to the
Soul and my ears are tuned to
Your Delightful Frequency!**

* * *

Day 17

He brought me up also out of an hor-
rible pit, out of the miry clay, and set my feet
upon a rock, and established my goings.

PSALM 40:2

Have you ever stepped in dog mess? Have you ever had an accident that required you to change clothes? Have you ever stated, "I need to get out of this mess?" Our emotional state can take us to a place that does not smell, look or feel good, but God is waiting on us to surrender the events surrounding our situations (mess) to Him. He wants us to forgive and forget. Have you ever come across the Scripture, "In his kindness, God called you to share in his eternal glory by means of Christ Jesus"? So, after you have suffered a little while (in your mess), He will restore, support, and strengthen you and will place you on a firm foundation. All power to Him forever!

Makeover Scriptures: Ephesians 3:14-21; 1 Peter 5:8-11

Timeless Beauty Tip #17:
You are ESTABLISHED!

❋ ❋ ❋

Today, I understand MY MESS is for a MOMENT!

❋ ❋ ❋

Let's Nail IT!

1. Describe the difficulty, distress, embarrassment (a messy situation) from which God had to extract you. Frequently, these are life events that did not go as we planned.

2. Describe a time when you were too emotional to make a righteous decision.

3. What did God promise to do for us when we are in this situation?

Polished Prayer:

Father God, forgive us for trying to understand and analyze everything. Lord, you see our condition, but now we take the time to verbalize it all to you, the one who can replenish, refresh, and renew. You can lift us out of the mire and place us upon a firm foundation where we may stand steadfast and secure. We take your hand as you pull us out; clean us up, restore, support and strengthen us as we walk ahead to only look back long enough to share the message of how you brought us out.

* * *

Despite what is going on around me, I am Standing Strong!!!!

* * *

Day 18

For the Lord taketh pleasure in his people: he will beautify the meek with salvation.

PSALM 149:4

While driving there are numerous things that can distract us: cell phones (texting/talking), external distractions (billboards/signs), listening to music, adjusting buttons, talking with the passengers and eating/drinking. In life, there are numerous things that can take our minds off of who we are in Christ Jesus and what Salvation has finished for us. The enemy loves it when he can distract us and get us to forget who we are in Christ Jesus. Often, when distracted while driving, we make mistakes like taking a wrong turn, driving too fast, staying idle too long, or forgetting where we were headed. The same things can happen in life.

Makeover Scriptures: Ephesians 1:3

Timeless Beauty Tip #18:
You are Dripping Beauty!

✳ ✳ ✳

✳ ✳ ✳

Let's Nail It!

1. List all the things that Salvation accomplished for us:

2. Write two to three of your favorite Scriptures about God's saving power:

3. Describe what your life was like before you were saved:

4. Write how Salvation has BEAUTIFIED YOU!

5. Confess if life has gotten you off course, then write your plans to get back on the road that God has destined for you:

Polished Prayer:

Lord, I thank you for your plan of salvation. You redeemed us from the path of destruction and reconciled us through your dear Son, Jesus Christ. You have forgiven us of all of our sins: past, present, and future, and we are grateful. You have freed us from a life of oppression, bondage, religion, laws, and striving for perfection in the sight of others. We belong to you; we are a part of a royal priesthood and are seated in heavenly place in Christ Jesus far above all principles, powers, and might. Forgive us for not embracing all that you have done for us, for forgetting who we are in Christ Jesus and for being easily distracted from the course you have predestined for us.

* * *

**Every day, I am BOLD,
BEAUTIFUL and SPIRITUALLY
BLESSED!!!**

* * *

Day 19

Happy is he that hath the God of Jacob for his help, whose hope is in the Lord his God.

PSALM 146:5

Have you ever had anyone fail you? If yes, raise your hand! These are the times you must believe that all things are working together for the good of those who are in Christ Jesus. There are times you must lean heavily on the truth that God will never leave you or forsake you. Overall, life is not all about us. Life is about what God is trying to do through us and learning to offer others the grace and love that Jesus offered to us when He died on the cross for our sins (mistakes). Finally, our hope should be in the Lord, not people. So take time to re-evaluate the event(s) in which you feel someone failed you, question whether or not your expectations (thoughts) were unrealistic for that person or situation. There are no perfect people.

Makeover Scriptures: Psalm 39:7; Psalm 62:5

Timeless Beauty Tip #19:
You are TICKLED PINK!

❀ ❀ ❀

Today, I chose to be CHIPPER, UPBEAT, and on CLOUD NINE!

❀ ❀ ❀

Let's Nail IT!

1. Briefly, revisit a recent event in which a person or people involved did not meet your expectation:

_____

_____

2. Write out your top five negative thoughts/emotions about the event:

    A. _____

    B. _____

    C. _____

    D. _____

    E. _____

3. Write out how you could have responded differently for each negative thought/emotion above:

    A. _____

    B. _____

    C. _____

D. _____

E. _____

4. Did you project your negative beliefs on others? For example, the event happened in the morning, but you took it out on someone that afternoon, or told everyone you encountered that day about your reactions to the event by badmouthing those involved before or without confronting the person who disappointed you? Matthew 18:15 tells if your brother shall trespass against you, go and tell him his fault between you and him alone; if he shall hear you, you have gained a brother.

5. Overall, did you take ownership of your own "stuff"? If you did so, what did you do? If not, what did you do?

Polished Prayer:

Lord, help us to love our neighbors as ourselves and to release our expectations of others to YOU. We give you the situations that make us want to cuss, fuss, and feel unjustly treated. As we choose to change, we ask for the power to quickly check ourselves and to walk peacefully away from disturbances knowing all things are working together for the good of those who are in Christ Jesus. We cast all of our cares upon you. Finally, teach us to offer the sacrifice of praise in all we do!

* * *

**Trusting You takes away
everything that seems Cloudy
and Blue!!!**

* * *

Day 20

And be not conformed to this world: but be ye transformed
by the renewing of your mind, that ye may prove what
is that good, and acceptable, and perfect, will of God.

ROMANS 12:2

Have you ever walked into an old office building? Have you walked through and seen the L shape of the building that reveals it has been remodeled a time or two? When it rains, you can smell the mold. During your lifetime you can recall a few minor facelifts, like when it was doctor's office and the decor was changed to olive green. Another small change was when the office got new black furniture for both lobby entrances with matching end tables, bookcases, and television stands. The last major overhaul was the when building received new paint, new carpet, and new baseboards. After the last major overhaul, that old office building went through a summer thunderstorm which revealed a leaking roof, windows, and doorways. This second remodeling experience reflects what happens spiritually in some of our lives. Sometimes we need a makeover because the first remodeling job just touched the surface of our problems. When a major disaster, life circumstances, separation, divorce, death or other traumatic event occurs, you discover if you can weather the storm.

Makeover Scriptures: Acts 27:1-44

Timeless Beauty Tip #20:
You are Teachable!

✻ ✻ ✻

Today, I am free to change; I am not a Copycat!

✻ ✻ ✻

Let's Nail It!

1. What have you been striving to change about yourself or others on your own?

A. _____

B. _____

C. _____

2. What have you learned about yourself during this 21-day challenge?

A. _____

B. _____

C. _____

D. _____

E. _____

3. What have you learned about the transforming power of God's Word?

A.

B.

C.

4. What have you learned about your prayer life?

A.

B.

C.

5. What have you learned about your self-esteem/personality?

A.

B.

C.

Polished Prayer:

Lord, forgive us for those times we imitated, mimicked others, and complied with the evils of this world. Allow the cleansing power of your Word to wash us from all impurities that have affected our personalities. Free us from bad choices, misguided friendships, bad life experiences, and inherited garbage. Remove all hindrances as we learn the truths that we can find hidden in your Word.

* * *

**Today, I decree and declare I
am an ORIGINAL DESIGN!**

* * *

Day 21

For we are his workmanship, created in Christ Jesus unto good works, which God hath before ordained that we should walk in them.

EPHESIANS 2:10

Recently, I had the opportunity to go with our church women's ministry to a painting class. The instructor stood in front of the class, illustrated, and gave step-by-step instructions while each woman diligently worked on her masterpiece. The outcome was a lady's pair of red pumps with the title, "Walking by Faith." There were approximately twenty women in the class, and no two pairs of red pumps looked alike. Some artists added diamonds to the shoe straps; others studded the pants legs, a few matched the color of the lady's foot to their skin tone, some ladies ripped the pant legs, others changed the original background from gray to orange. One lady made her masterpiece look like an illusion. The art shows that, although we all serve one living God, we who created masterpieces all over the world, we are all individually crafted for His purpose.

Makeover Scriptures: 2 Corinthians 5:17

Timeless Beauty Tip #21
You are a Masterpiece!

❃ ❃ ❃

Today, I embrace my Uniqueness!

❃ ❃ ❃

Let's Nail IT!

1. What qualities and characteristics make you unique?

    A. _____

    B. _____

    C. _____

2. What goal(s) have you been actively pursuing?

    A. _____

    B. _____

    C. _____

3. Have you asked God for the good things He has planned for you? If yes, briefly write the answer after seeking God for the answers for your future.

Polished Prayer:

Lord, I thank you for what you have called and purposed us to do. We are not perfect but chosen. Rid us of images of ourselves that do not reflect YOU: low self-esteem, insecurities, and a passel of hang-ups. After YOU created everything in the heavens and on earth, YOU said, "It is GOOD." Forgive us for seeing ourselves as weak, helpless, and hopeless. As we arise, let us stay on course with your perfect will. Reveal to us the good things you have planned and purpose for us.

* * *

I decree and declare I am HIS Masterpiece!

* * *

Add a Little
More Color!

This book of the law shall not depart out of thy mouth; but thou shalt meditate therein day and night, that thou mayest observe to do according to all that is written therein: for then thou shalt make thy way prosperous, and then thou shalt have good success. Have not I commanded thee? Be strong and of a good courage; be not afraid, neither be thou dismayed: for the Lord thy God is with thee whithersoever thou goest.

JOSHUA 1:8-9

Let this mind be in you, which was also is Christ Jesus.

PHILIPPIANS 2:5

For I know the thoughts that I think toward you, saith the LORD, thoughts of peace, and not of evil to give you an expected end.

JEREMIAH 29:11

But they that wait upon the LORD shall renew [their] strength; they shall mount up with wings as eagles; they shall run, and not be weary; [and] they shall walk, and not faint.

ISAIAH 40:31

GIVE ME BEAUTY

Testimony

GOD'S GLOWING RESULT!!! Read Daniel, chapter 1 and chapter 10 to learn about the results of these times of fasting and praying.

For the past 21 days, you and or your small group have been searching the Scriptures, fasting and praying, to gain a greater revelation of God's view of Beauty. You are at the end of your journey.

Now write a brief testimony of your experience to include moving forward from the ashes of your life with a new perspective and new goals to accomplish.

If you wrote a testimony, I would love for you to take a moment to post your story on my Facebook page, www.facebook.com/cynthia.f.albert

Facilitator's *Guide*

Give Me Beauty – 21 Day Challenge Objectives:

- To build relationships by having a time of fellowship
- To promote Christian maturity
- To deepen our understanding of Scripture
- To create an atmosphere that encourages prayer and seeking God for the healing, we desperately desire
- To encourage leadership skills

Facilitator's Role:

- To be a role model for studying God's Word and for prayer
- To plan time, location, and light refreshments
- To disciple the members by encouraging them to be Christ-like by providing sound doctrine and avoid trying to fix the members
- To ensure that time is well spent
- To hold the group accountable for attendance, daily Scripture reading, to answer questions to the best of your ability, to pray, and to spend time in God's presence
- To promote transformation by the power meditating on Scripture, of prayer, of fasting, and of declaring God's Word over our lives and situations

- To protect the atmosphere by ensuring confidentiality. Whatever happens in the sessions stays in the sessions
- To identify potential leaders

Purpose: To develop a lifestyle of tearing down self-defeating thoughts, seeking and practicing forgiveness, focusing on our potential and being empowered by declaring God's Word over our lives.

Group Size: 3 to 12 women, ages 18 and up

Meeting Time/Meeting Space: Schedule the meeting days, time, location (church, home, conference call, Skype, etc.). Three to five weekly meetings for a one-hour discussion is recommended.

SAMPLE MEETING #1 FORMAT

Introductions - (3-5 minutes)

Prayer - (5 minutes) - Facilitator will ask God to bless each attendee and to minister by the power of the Holy Spirit to individual needs. (3-5 minutes)

Introductions/icebreaker/empowering praise and worship or testimonies

Confidentiality and Small Group Ground Rules - (10 minutes) - List of rules the group develops and hold each attendee accountable for upholding.

Biblical foundation - (20 minutes) - As a group, review Scriptures regarding Asking God and the results of Fasting - (15 minutes Session 1 only). Encourage women who have never fasted to try a one or three-day a week partial fast by eating fruits, nuts, and grains only, if they are healthy or cleared by their medical practitioner. Those who are more experienced could try the full 21 days of fasting.

A fasting handout has been included to aid the facilitator, along with a list a Bible verses pertaining to fasting. All other sessions will focus on the Scriptures studied during the previous week.

Encourage Daily Scripture reading, self-exploration, and prayer: Read the next seven days, answer the questions, and prepare to participate in the discussion at the next session. (Sessions 2-4 only)

Testimony - (Session 5 only) Each woman will write a testimony, create a vision board, write a poem, and share by other creative expression what God has done in their life because of the GIVE ME BEAUTY 21 DAY CHALLENGE.

Close each session with prayer.

* * *

Facilitator should follow up with each woman individually weekly with a 5-minute call and offer additional support/prayer as needed.

* * *

Fasting
Bible Verses

And he was there with the LORD forty days and forty nights; he did neither eat bread, nor drink water. And he wrote upon the tables the words of the covenant, the Ten Commandments.

EXODUS 34:28

Go, gather together all the Jews that are present in Shushan, and fast ye for me, and neither eat nor drink three days, night or day: I also and my maidens will fast likewise; and so will I go in unto the king, which is not according to the law: and if I perish, I perish.

ESTHER 4:16

And they mourned, and wept, and fasted until even, for Saul, and for Jonathan his son, and for the people of the Lord, and for the house of Israel; because they were fallen by the sword.

2 SAMUEL 1:12

Then said the Lord unto me, Pray not for this people for their good.

When they fast, I will not hear their cry; and when they offer burnt offering and an oblation, I will not accept them: but I will consume them by the sword, and by the famine, and by the pestilence.

JEREMIAH 14:11-12

"Cry loudly, do not hold back; Raise your voice like a trumpet, And declare to My people their transgression And to the house of Jacob their sins. Yet they seek Me day by day and delight to know My ways, As a nation that has done righteousness And has not forsaken the ordinance of their God They ask Me for just decisions, They delight in the nearness of God. 'Why have we fasted and You do not see? Why have we humbled ourselves and You do not notice? Behold, on the day of your fast you find your desire, And drive hard all your workers.

ISAIAH 58:1-7

Then the word of the LORD of hosts came to me, saying, "Say to all the people of the land and to the priests, 'When you fasted and mourned in the fifth and seventh months these seventy years, was it actually for Me that you fasted?' When you eat and drink, do you not eat for yourselves and do you not drink for yourselves?"

ZECHARIAH 7:4-7

Whenever you fast, do not put on a gloomy face as the hypocrites do, for they neglect their appearance so that they will be noticed by men when they are fasting Truly I say to you, they have their reward in full. But you, when you fast, anoint your head and wash your face so that your fasting will not be noticed by men, but by your Father who is in secret; and your Father who sees what is done in secret will reward you.

MATTHEW 6:16-18

Then the disciples of John came to Him, asking, "Why do we and the Pharisees fast, but your disciples do not fast?" And Jesus said to them, "The attendants of the bridegroom cannot mourn as long as the bridegroom is with them, can they? But the days will come when the bridegroom is taken away from them, and then they will fast."

MATTHEW 9:14-15

John's disciples and the Pharisees were fasting; and they came and said to Him, "Why do John's disciples and the disciples of the Pharisees fast, but your disciples do not fast?" And Jesus said to them, "While the bridegroom is with them, the attendants of the bridegroom cannot fast, can they? So long as they have the bridegroom with them, they cannot fast. But the days will come when the bridegroom is taken away from them, and then they will fast in that day."

MARK 2:18-20

And they said to Him, "The disciples of John often fast and offer prayers, the disciples of the Pharisees also do the same, but yours eat and drink." And Jesus said to them, "You cannot make the attendants of the bridegroom fast while the bridegroom is with them, can you? But the days will come; and when the bridegroom is taken away from them, then they will fast in those days."

LUKE 5:33-35

Now the men of Israel were hard-pressed on that day, for Saul had put the people under oath, saying, "Cursed be the man who eats food before evening, and until I have avenged myself on my enemies." So none of the people tasted food. All the people of the land entered the forest, and there was honey on the ground. When the people entered the forest, behold, there was a flow of honey; but no man put his hand to his mouth, for the people feared the oath.

1 SAMUEL 14:24-30

But as for me, when they were sick, my clothing was sackcloth; I humbled my soul with fasting, And my prayer kept returning to my bosom.

PSALM 35:13

It came about when Ahab heard these words, that he tore his clothes and put on sackcloth and fasted, and he lay in sackcloth and went about despondently. Then the word of the LORD came to Elijah the Tishbite, saying, "Do you see how Ahab has humbled himself before Me? Because he has humbled himself before Me, I will not bring the evil in his days, but I will bring the evil upon his house in his son 's days."

1 KINGS 21:27-29

Then I proclaimed a fast there at the river of Ahava, that we might humble ourselves before our God to seek from Him a safe journey for us, our little ones, and all our possessions.

EZRA 8:21

When I wept in my soul with fasting, It became my reproach.

PSALM 69:10

They gathered to Mizpah, and drew water and poured it out before the LORD, and fasted on that day and said there, "We have sinned against the LORD." And Samuel judged the sons of Israel at Mizpah.

1 SAMUEL 7:6

Now on the twenty-fourth day of this month the sons of Israel assembled with fasting, in sackcloth and with dirt upon them. The descendants of Israel separated themselves from all foreigners, and stood and confessed their sins and the iniquities of their fathers. While they stood in their place, they read from the book of the law of the LORD their God for a fourth of the day; and for another fourth they confessed and worshiped the LORD their God.

NEHEMIAH 9:1-3

Gird yourselves with sackcloth And lament, O priests; Wail, O ministers of the altar! Come, spend the night in sackcloth O ministers of my God, For the grain offering and the drink offering Are withheld from the house of your God. Consecrate a fast, Proclaim a solemn assembly; Gather the elders And all the inhabitants of the land To the house of the LORD your God, And cry out to the LORD.

JOEL 1:13-14

"Yet even now," declares the LORD, "Return to Me with all your heart, And with fasting, weeping and mourning; And rend your heart and not your garments Now return to the LORD your God, For He is gracious and compassionate, Slow to anger, abounding in lovingkindness And relenting of evil. Who knows whether He will not turn and relent And leave a blessing behind Him, Even a grain offering and a drink offering For the LORD your God?"

JOEL 2:12-15

When I heard these words, I sat down and wept and mourned for days; and I was fasting and praying before the God of heaven.

NEHEMIAH 1:4

Then I proclaimed a fast there at the river of Ahava, that we might humble ourselves before our God to seek from Him a safe journey for us, our little ones, and all our possessions. For I was ashamed to request from the king troops and horsemen to protect us from the enemy on the way, because we had said to the king, "The hand of our God is favorably disposed to all those who seek Him, but His power and His anger are against all those who forsake Him." So we fasted and sought our God concerning this matter, and He listened to our entreaty.

EZRA 8:21-23

So I gave my attention to the Lord God to seek Him by prayer and supplications, with fasting, sackcloth and ashes.

DANIEL 9:3

And He said to them, "Because of the littleness of your faith; for truly I say to you, if you have faith the size of a mustard seed, you will say to this mountain, 'Move from here to there,' and it will move; and nothing will be impossible to you."

MATTHEW 17:20

And He said to them, "This kind cannot come out by anything but prayer."

MARK 9:29

...and then as a widow to the age of eighty-four. She never left the temple, serving night and day with fastings and prayers.

LUKE 2:37

And they said to Him, "The disciples of John often fast and offer prayers, the disciples of the Pharisees also do the same, but yours eat and drink."

LUKE 5:33

Then, when they had fasted and prayed and laid their hands on them, they sent them away.

ACTS 13:3

When they had appointed elders for them in every church, having prayed with fasting, they commended them to the Lord in whom they had believed.

ACTS 14:23

The husband must fulfill his duty to his wife, and likewise also the wife to her husband. The wife does not have authority over her own body, but the husband does; and likewise also the husband does not have authority over his own body, but the wife does. Stop depriving one another, except by agreement for a time, so that you may devote yourselves to prayer, and come together again so that Satan will not tempt you because of your lack of self-control.

1 CORINTHIANS 7:3-5

While they were ministering to the Lord and fasting, the Holy Spirit said, "Set apart for Me Barnabas and Saul for the work to which I have called them."

ACTS 13:2

Four Types of Fast
According to Scripture

Regular - Matthew 4:1-11

Partial - Daniel 10:12

Full - Acts 9:9; Esther 4:15-16

Sexual - 1 Corinthians 7:3-6

As you review the Scriptures on the four types of fasting, look at what they abstain from, the type of opposition they face, and the outcome of their sacrifice.

Timeless Beauty *Tips*

Timeless Beauty Tip #1:
You are CROWNED with BEAUTY!

Timeless Beauty Tip #2:
Your MIND belongs to Christ!

Timeless Beauty Tip #3:
You are SHINING!

Timeless Beauty Tip #4:
You are GENTLE, QUIET, and SUBMITTED!

Timeless Beauty Tip #5:
You are RADIANT!

Timeless Beauty Tip #6:
You are WORSHIP!

Timeless Beauty Tip # 7:
You are KNITTED TOGETHER!

Timeless Beauty Tip #8:
You are ON TIME!

Timeless Beauty Tip #9:
You are CLEAN!

Timeless Beauty Tip #10:
You are CLOTHED IN LOVE!

Timeless Beauty Tip #11:
You are WISE!

Timeless Beauty Tip #12:
You are DISCREET!

Timeless Beauty Tip #13:
You are SUFFICIENT!

Timeless Beauty Tip #14:
You are ATTRACTIVE!

Timeless Beauty Tip #15:
You are Priceless!

Timeless Beauty Tip #16:
Your FLOW IS FLAWLESS!

Timeless Beauty Tip #17:
You are ESTABLISHED!

Timeless Beauty Tip #18:
You are Dripping Beauty!

Timeless Beauty Tip #19:
You are TICKLED PINK!

Timeless Beauty Tip #20:
You are Teachable!

Timeless Beauty Tip #21:
You are a Masterpiece!

The Author

CYNTHIA FORREST ALBERT was born and raised in Marianna, Florida to Mr. Charles and Jean (Williams) Forrest. At a young age she gave her life to Christ and began to serve faithfully at New Mt. Olive Baptist Church as an Usher, Sunday School Secretary, and Youth Choir member. She continued the journey of servanthood at Pentecostal Worship Center, in Panama City, Florida under the tutelage of Bishop J.W. Wade, II, and Pastor Marie Wade. Over the past fourteen years, Cynthia has served in leadership positions as Parish Pastor, New Member Instructor, Cell Group Coordinator, Senior Adjutant, Assistant Pastor of Administration, along with training and developing others for the Kingdom.

She is a graduate of Florida State University with a Bachelor of Science in Psychology and earned a Master of Science degree in Counseling and Psychology graduate from Troy State University-Dothan. In addition, she has over twenty-five years of experience counseling and encouraging vulnerable populations: incarcerated, poor, hungry, elderly, homeless, uninsured, mentally ill, abused, and children and adults suffering from a range of chronic diseases including those individuals infected and/or affected by HIV/AIDS.

Cynthia Albert has three children: Shae, Donovan, and Jeremy, who have blessed her with seven grandchildren. She loves encouraging other women through prayer, small group Bible studies, and one-on-one mentoring. Her heartfelt passion is to see others reach their full potential in Christ Jesus.

In 2013 Cynthia was faced with various life challenges: separation followed by divorce, loss of a home, low self-esteem, betrayal, hurt, pain, financial difficulty, family disunity, depression and more. During this dark season she leaned heavily upon the Lord, searching for answers, strength and purpose through private Bible study, fasting, praying, and finding comfort among other Christian women. Through these tests, she has given birth to this Bible study with more books to follow. Cynthia's goal is to inspire the world, one book at a time, through her writings.

Let's stay connected!
www.facebook.com/cynthia.f.albert

To inquire about Cynthia facilitating a *Give Me Beauty* Session for your church, small group, outreach ministry or Women's Ministry contact (850) 329-5488.

9 780999 978441 9